I Love My Pet
TURTLE

Alexis Roumanis

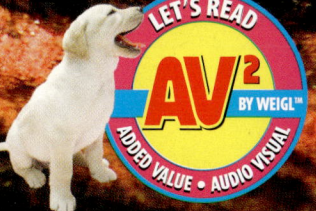

www.av2books.com

AV² provides enriched content that supplements and complements this book. Weigl's AV² books strive to create inspired learning and engage young minds in a total learning experience.

Your AV² Media Enhanced books come alive with...

 **Audio** Listen to sections of the book read aloud.

 **Video** Watch informative video clips.

 **Embedded Weblinks** Gain additional information for research.

Try This! Complete activities and hands-on experiments.

 **Key Words** Study vocabulary, and complete a matching word activity.

 **Quizzes** Test your knowledge.

 **Slide Show** View images and captions, and prepare a presentation.

... and much, much more!

Go to www.av2books.com, and enter this book's unique code.

BOOK CODE

B526653

AV² by Weigl brings you media enhanced books that support active learning.

Published by AV² by Weigl
350 5th Avenue, 59th Floor   New York, NY 10118
Websites: www.av2books.com   www.weigl.com

Copyright ©2015 AV² by Weigl
All rights reserved. No part of this publication may be reproduced, stored in a retrieval system, or transmitted in any form or by any means, electronic, mechanical, photocopying, recording, or otherwise, without the prior permission of the publisher.

  Library of Congress Control Number: 2014934860
ISBN 978-1-4896-1306-6 (hardcover)
ISBN 978-1-4896-1307-3 (softcover)
ISBN 978-1-4896-1308-0 (single-user eBook)
ISBN 978-1-4896-1309-7 (multi-user eBook)

Printed in the United States of America in North Mankato, Minnesota
1 2 3 4 5 6 7 8 9 0   18 17 16 15 14

042014
WEP150314

Senior Editor: Aaron Carr   Art Director: Terry Paulhus

Weigl acknowledges Getty Images as the primary image supplier for this title.

I Love My Pet
TURTLE

CONTENTS

- 2 AV² Book Code
- 4 Turtles
- 6 Life Cycle
- 10 Features
- 14 Care
- 20 Health
- 22 Turtle Facts
- 24 Key Words
- 24 www.av2books.com

I love my pet turtle.
I take good care of her.

My pet turtle hatched from an egg. She could swim right after hatching.

7

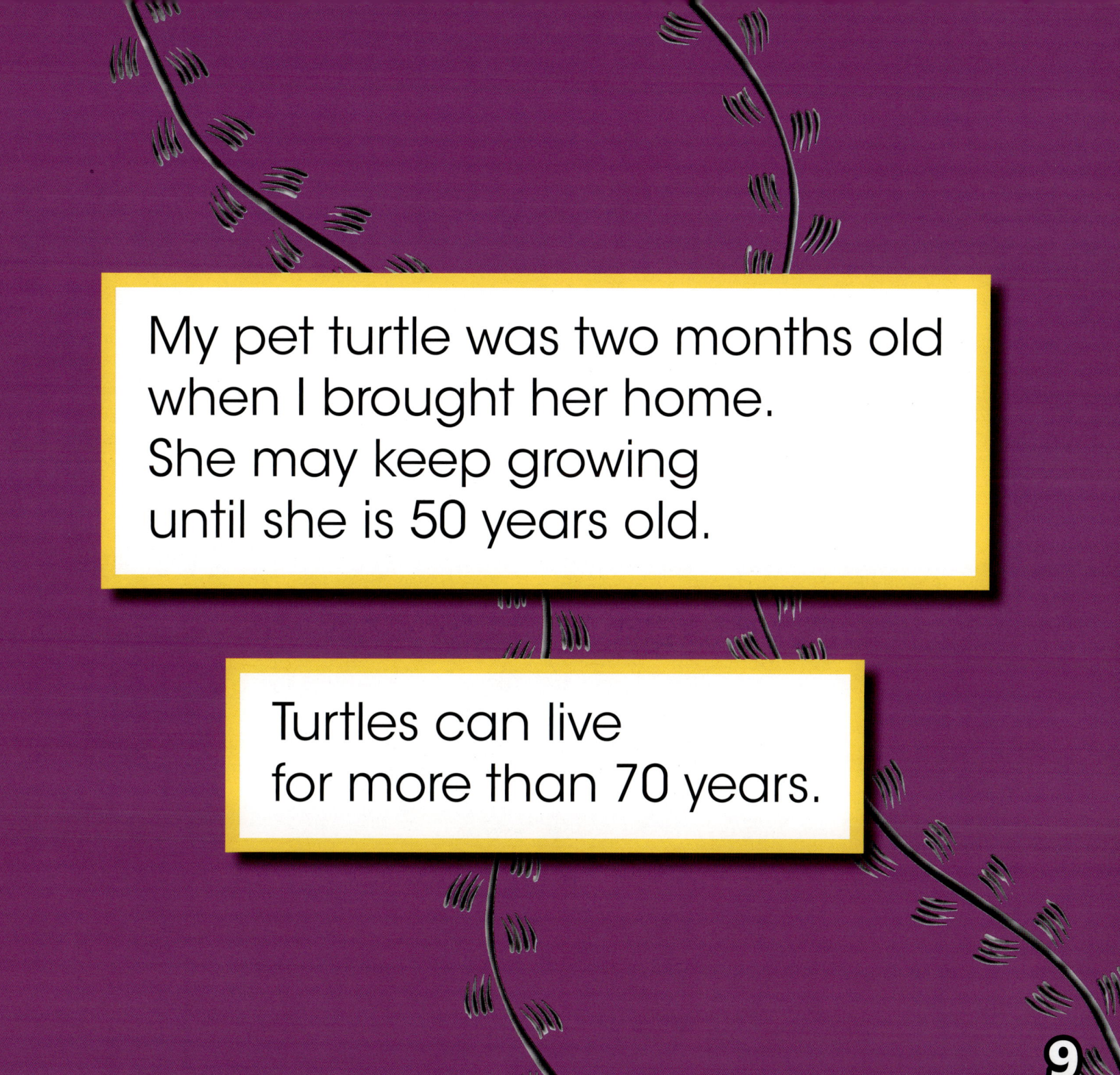

My pet turtle was two months old when I brought her home.
She may keep growing until she is 50 years old.

Turtles can live for more than 70 years.

My pet turtle sleeps through the winter. She can stay asleep for a few weeks.

My pet turtle has a hard shell on her back.
Her shell helps to keep her safe.

Some turtles can hide their heads in their shells.

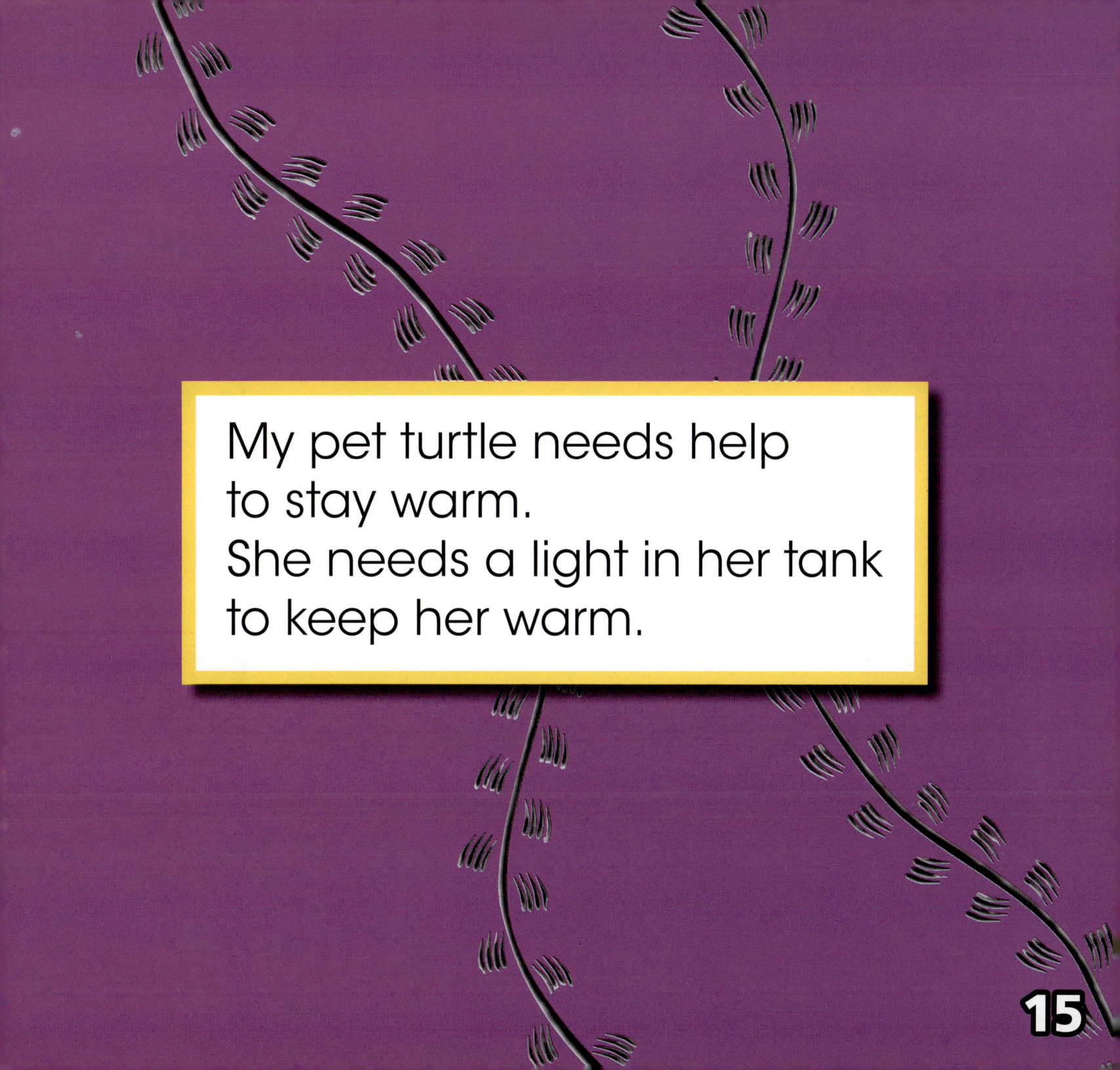

My pet turtle needs help to stay warm.
She needs a light in her tank to keep her warm.

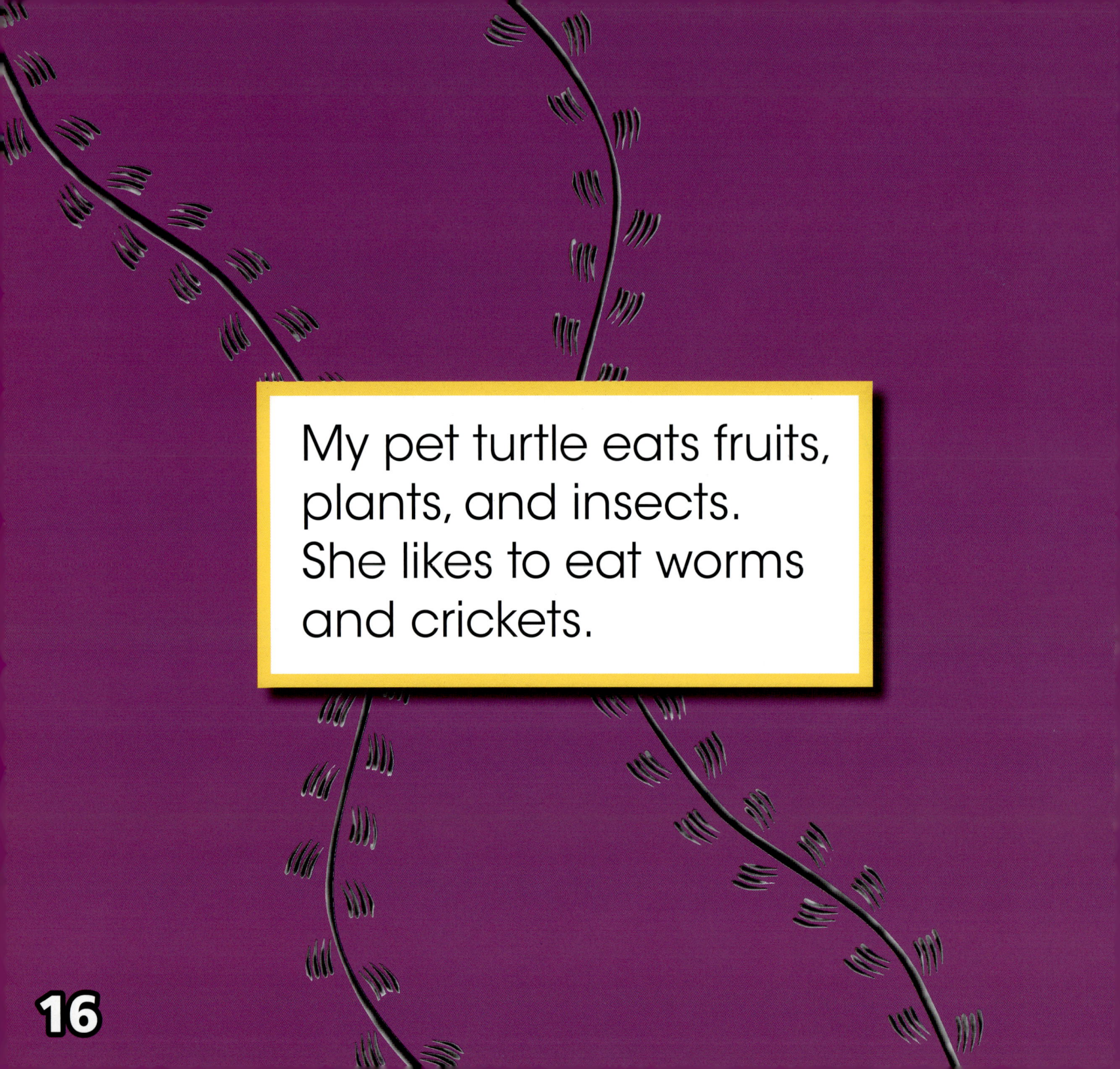

My pet turtle eats fruits, plants, and insects. She likes to eat worms and crickets.

My pet turtle needs to be cared for. Her water needs to be changed every day.

I make sure my pet turtle is healthy.
I love my pet turtle.

TURTLE FACTS

These pages provide more detail about the interesting facts found in the book. They are intended to be used by adults as a learning support to help young readers round out their knowledge of each animal featured in the *I Love My Pet* series.

Pages 4–5

I love my pet turtle. I take good care of her. There are about 300 kinds of turtles and tortoises. Turtles like to live in water, while tortoises live on land. Most turtle owners keep the red-eared slider turtle as pets. Turtles need regular care to stay happy and healthy. They need a clean tank, food, water, and exercise. Although turtles may seem easy to care for, they need time and effort on a regular basis to stay healthy.

Pages 6–7

My pet turtle hatched from an egg. She could swim right after hatching. Turtles are reptiles. Reptiles lay eggs to have babies. When turtles hatch from their eggs, they are called hatchlings. Turtles use a temporary tooth to break out of their eggs. Turtle hatchlings can move around on their own right after hatching. Many turtles try to find water as soon as they leave their nests.

Pages 8–9

My pet turtle was two months old when I brought her home. She may keep growing until she is 50 years old. Most turtles are ready to live with their new owners when they are several weeks old. A turtle's lifespan varies depending on the species. This is also true for their size. The largest turtle ever recorded was a leatherback turtle that measured 9 feet (3 meters) long.

Pages 10–11

My pet turtle sleeps through the winter. She can stay asleep for a few weeks. Many turtles will sleep when it is cold and dark. This is called hibernation. Turtles can hibernate for about 10 to 20 weeks. It is important to talk with a veterinarian to see if a turtle should hibernate. A turtle will only hibernate if it is not fed for several days. Then, a pet owner must place the turtle tank in a dark place.

Pages 12–13  **My pet turtle has a hard shell on her back. Her shell helps to keep her safe.** The shell is a turtle's main defense against predators. The shell is part of a turtle's body. It has openings for the legs, head, and tail. When a predator approaches, the turtle can pull its head, legs, and tail into the shell to keep them safe. Some turtles, such as the snapping turtle, have other ways of protecting themselves. These turtles can attack predators with a strong bite.

Pages 14–15  **My pet turtle needs help to stay warm. She needs a light in her tank to keep her warm.** As a cold blooded animal, turtles cannot make their own heat to stay warm. Instead, turtles must sit in sunlight to heat up or dip in water to cool off. A pet turtle needs a special heat light in its tank. The tank needs a thermometer, as the exact temperature of the tank needs to be controlled.

Pages 16–17  **My pet turtle eats fruits, plants, and bugs. She also likes to eat worms and crickets.** Young turtles need to be fed at least once a day. Adult turtles need to be fed at least three times per week. Young turtles should eat meals that are about 50 to 70 percent meat. Adults only need to eat meals that are about 10 to 20 percent meat. The rest of their food can be a mixture of leaves, fruit, and vegetables.

Pages 18–19  **My pet turtle needs to be cared for. Her water needs to be changed every day.** Turtles need a lot of water for swimming. Usually, a tank should have 10 gallons (38 liters) of water for each inch (2.5 centimeters) of the turtle's length. A water pump and filter are needed to keep the tank water clean. Turtles also need to be able to climb out of their water onto a rock to get warm.

Pages 20–21  **I help make sure my pet turtle is healthy. I love my pet turtle.** Keeping a turtle healthy and happy is a big job. Regularly replacing some of the water in a tank will help to keep a turtle healthy. It may be helpful to remove a turtle from its tank before it eats. This will help keep water in the tank clean. To stay safe, pet owners should always wash their hands after cleaning a tank or touching a turtle.

KEY WORDS

Research has shown that as much as 65 percent of all written material published in English is made up of 300 words. These 300 words cannot be taught using pictures or learned by sounding them out. They must be recognized by sight. This book contains 54 common sight words to help young readers improve their reading fluency and comprehension. This book also teaches young readers several important content words, such as proper nouns. These words are paired with pictures to aid in learning and improve understanding.

Page	Sight Words First Appearance
4	good, her, I, my, of, take
6	after, an, could, from, right, she
9	can, for, home, is, keep, live, may, more, old, than, two, until, was, when, years
11	a, few, the, through
12	back, hard, has, heads, helps, in, on, some, their, to
15	light, needs
16	also, and, eats, likes, plants
18	be, changed, day, every, water
21	make

Page	Content Words First Appearance
4	turtle
6	egg
9	months
11	weeks, winter
12	safe, shell
15	tank
16	bugs, crickets, fruits, worms

Check out www.av2books.com for activities, videos, audio clips, and more!

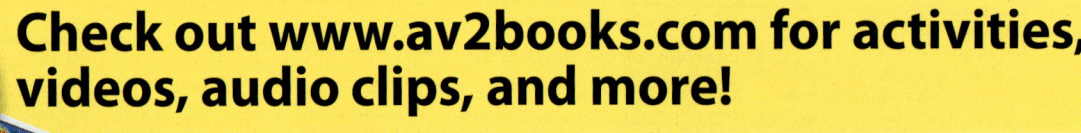
 Go to www.av2books.com.
 Enter book code.   B526653
 Fuel your imagination online!

www.av2books.com